Englisch hören und lesen
Für Grundschulkinder

The Adventures of Pinocchio

Pinocchios Abenteuer

Schwager & Steinlein

Geppetto is
a poor carpenter and
he has no children.
One day he takes
a strange
piece of wood
and makes a puppet.

He makes
a head and
two eyes, …

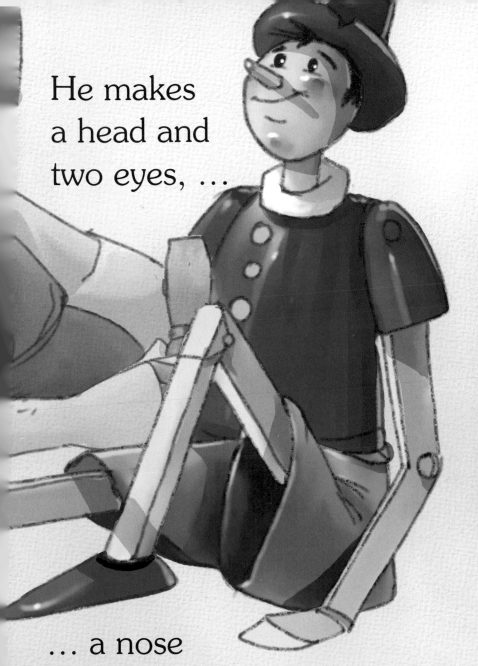

… a nose
and a mouth, two arms, two
hands, two legs and two feet.

Immediately the puppet
starts jumping around.
Geppetto is very happy.
The puppet is
his son now!

– You must go to school, but first you need a name – Geppetto says. – I can call you Pinocchio.

Geppetto goes out
and sells his coat
to buy a spelling
book.

At home Pinocchio hears a voice: – Hello, I'm Jiminy Cricket. Be good to Geppetto: he is a good man!

7

Geppetto gives Pinocchio
the spelling book. – Go to
school and be a good boy!

Pinocchio leaves the house
with his spelling book
and …

… Jiminy Cricket follows him.

On the way Pinocchio hears some music and he sells his spelling book to buy a ticket for Fire Eater's Puppet Show.

Soon he's on stage singing and dancing with all the other puppets.

The show is a success
and Fire Eater wants
Pinocchio to stay.

– Remember that Geppetto
wants you to go to school –
says Jiminy Cricket.

13

Luckily Fire Eater knows Geppetto and gives Pinocchio five pieces of gold to take to him.

– I want to buy Geppetto
a new coat with this
money! – says Pinocchio.

On the way home he meets
a cat and a fox and he tells
them about his good fortune.
– You can make more
money if you come
with us – says the cat.

– Where? – asks Pinocchio.
– To our magic field – the
fox says. – You bury the
money and you have
a tree of gold the next day.

– No, Pinocchio,
that money is for
Geppetto – cries Jiminy
Cricket. But Pinocchio
goes to the magic field
and he buries the money.

The next day
he goes to the field
but there's no tree of gold.
There's only an empty
hole!

The money is not there!
He starts crying.

Near the field lives the
Blue Fairy. She hears
Pinocchio crying and she
goes to see what's wrong.

– There's a hole in my
pocket. The money
I want to take to
Geppetto is not here! –
cries Pinocchio.

But suddenly his nose
begins to grow.
– Are you sure? Don't lie.
Where is your money? –
the Blue Fairy asks.

– I don't know. It's not
in my pocket anymore! –
replies Pinocchio.
His nose goes on growing.

The Blue Fairy laughs: – When
you tell a lie, your nose grows!
So Pinocchio promises not
to tell any more lies.

– Go home and be
a good boy! – the
Blue Fairy says.
Pinocchio thanks the
Fairy and runs home.

But on the way he meets a boy. – Come to the Land of Toys with me! – he says. – Nobody goes to school there and you can play all day long!

– Don't listen to him –
says Jiminy Cricket.

– We can take the carriage
this evening – says
the boy.

Pinocchio forgets all the
promises to his father
and to the Fairy. They
jump up in the carriage
to the Land of Toys.

– Life is great here!
No books, no lessons and
we can play all the time! –
cries Pinocchio.

One day Pinocchio
notices he has
long, hairy ears …

32

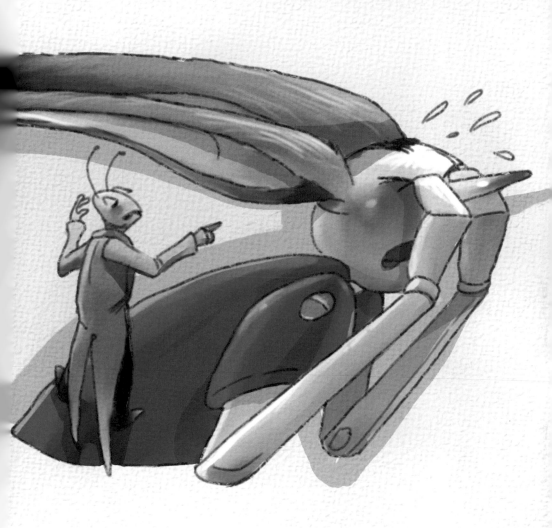

– You are turning into
a donkey! – says Jiminy
Cricket. – I want to go
home! – cries Pinocchio.

– Jump into the sea
and escape from here! –
says Jiminy Cricket.

So they jump into the
dark sea and swim in the
waves.

Then they see a light
in the dark.

They swim and swim
right into the whale's mouth.
– We are inside a whale! –
cries Jiminy Cricket.

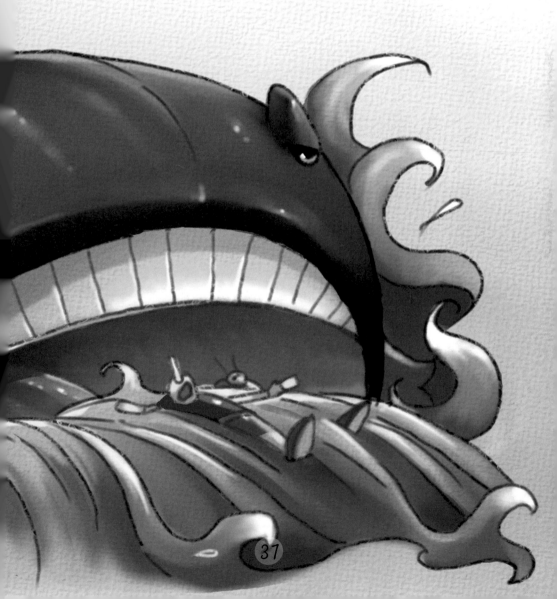

– Pinocchio! – a voice calls.
– What? But it's you,
dad! – cries Pinocchio
so happy to see
Geppetto.

– We must get out of here
and swim to land! –
Pinocchio says.
When the whale opens its
mouth they get out.

Pinocchio swims
and pulls Geppetto.
When they reach
dry land, they are
very tired.

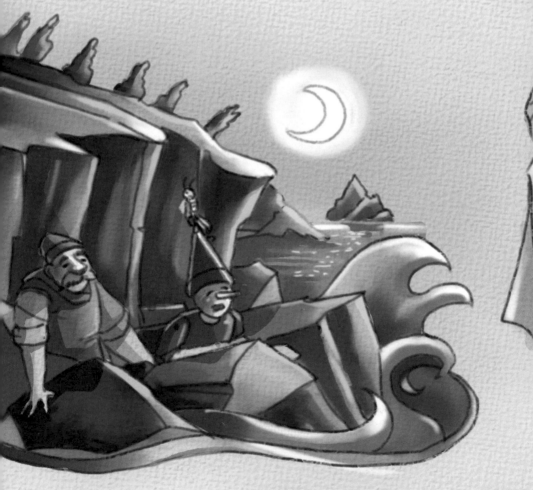

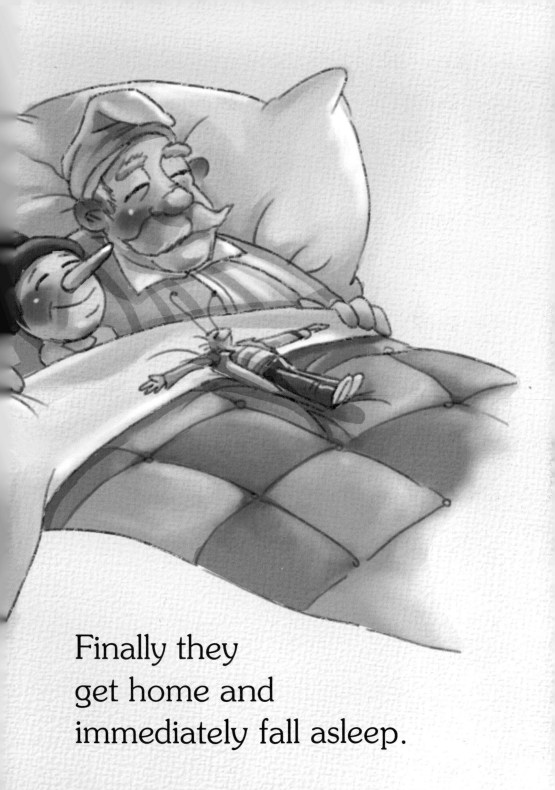

Finally they
get home and
immediately fall asleep.

The next day they
wake up and the Blue
Fairy is there.
– Look in the mirror! –
she says to Pinocchio.

Pinocchio is a real boy with blue eyes and brown hair.
– Oh, my son! – cries Geppetto with joy.

– You are a good boy:
this is your reward! –
says the Blue Fairy.

Pinocchio and Geppetto
are very happy and they
jump and laugh together!

The Adventures of Pinocchio

Pinocchios Abenteuer

Seite 2

Geppetto is a poor carpenter and he has no children.
One day he takes a strange piece of wood and makes a puppet.

Geppetto ist ein armer Tischler, und er hat keine Kinder.
Eines Tages nimmt er ein seltsames Stück Holz und macht eine Puppe.

Seite 3

He makes a head and two eyes, … a nose and a mouth,
two arms, two hands, two legs and two feet.

Er macht einen Kopf und zwei Augen, … eine Nase und einen Mund,
zwei Arme, zwei Hände, zwei Beine und zwei Füße.

Seite 4

Immediately the puppet starts jumping around.
Geppetto is very happy. The puppet is his son now!

Sofort beginnt die Puppe herumzuhüpfen.
Geppetto ist sehr glücklich. Die Puppe ist jetzt sein Sohn!

Seite 5

– You must go to school, but first you need a name – Geppetto says.
– I can call you Pinocchio.

– Du musst zur Schule gehen, aber erst brauchst du einen Namen –
sagt Geppetto.
– Ich kann dich Pinocchio nennen.

Seite 6

Geppetto goes out and sells his coat to buy a spelling book.

Geppetto geht los und verkauft seine Jacke, um ein ABC-Buch
zu kaufen.

Seite 7

At home Pinocchio hears a voice: – Hello, I'm Jiminy Cricket. Be good
to Geppetto: he is a good man!

Zu Hause hört Pinocchio eine Stimme: – Hallo, ich bin Jiminy Grille.
Sei gut zu Geppetto: Er ist ein guter Mann!

Seite 8

Geppetto gives Pinocchio the spelling book. – Go to school and be a
good boy!
Pinocchio leaves the house with his spelling book and …

Geppetto gibt Pinocchio das ABC-Buch. – Geh zur Schule und sei
ein guter Junge!
Pinocchio verlässt mit seinem ABC-Buch das Haus und …

Seite 9

… Jiminy Cricket follows him.

… Jiminy Grille folgt ihm.

Seite 10

On the way Pinocchio hears some music and he sells his spelling book to
buy a ticket for Fire Eater's Puppet Show.

Auf dem Weg hört Pinocchio Musik, und er verkauft sein ABC-Buch,
um eine Eintrittskarte für Feuerfressers Puppentheater zu kaufen.

Seite 11

Soon he's on stage singing and dancing with all the other puppets.

Bald ist er auf der Bühne, singt und tanzt mit all den anderen Puppen.

Seite 12

The show is a success and Fire Eater wants Pinocchio to stay.

Die Vorstellung ist ein Erfolg, und Feuerfresser will, dass Pinocchio bleibt.

Seite 13

– Remember that Geppetto wants you to go to school – says Jiminy Cricket.

– Denk daran, Geppetto will, dass du zur Schule gehst – sagt Jiminy Grille.

Seite 14

Luckily Fire Eater knows Geppetto and gives Pinocchio five pieces of gold to take to him.

Zum Glück kennt Feuerfresser Geppetto und gibt Pinocchio fünf Goldstücke für ihn mit.

Seite 15

– I want to buy Geppetto a new coat with this money! – says Pinocchio.

– Ich will Geppetto von diesem Geld eine neue Jacke kaufen! – sagt Pinocchio.

Seite 16

On the way home he meets a cat and a fox and he tells them about his good fortune. – You can make more money if you come with us – says the cat.

Auf dem Heimweg trifft er einen Kater und einen Fuchs, und er erzählt ihnen von seinem Glück. – Du kannst noch mehr Geld verdienen, wenn du mit uns kommst – sagt der Kater.

Seite 17

– Where? – asks Pinocchio. – To our magic field – the fox says.
– You bury the money and you have a tree of gold the next day.

– Wohin? – fragt Pinocchio. – Zu unserem Wunderfeld – sagt der Fuchs.
– Du vergräbst das Geld, und am nächsten Tag hast du einen Baum
aus Gold.

Seite 18

– No, Pinocchio, that money is for Geppetto – cries Jiminy Cricket.
But Pinocchio goes to the magic field and he buries the money.

– Nein, Pinocchio, das Geld ist für Geppetto – schreit Jiminy Grille.
Aber Pinocchio geht zu dem Wunderfeld, und er vergräbt das Geld.

Seite 19

The next day he goes to the field but there's no tree of gold.
There's only an empty hole!

Am nächsten Tag geht er zu dem Feld, aber da ist kein Baum aus Gold.
Da ist nur ein leeres Loch!

Seite 20

The money is not there! He starts crying.

Das Geld ist nicht da! Er fängt an zu weinen.

Seite 21

Near the field lives the Blue Fairy.
She hears Pinocchio crying and she goes to see what's wrong.

Nahe dem Feld lebt die Blaue Fee.
Sie hört Pinocchio weinen, und sie geht nachsehen, was los ist.

Seite 22

– There's a hole in my pocket. The money I want to take to Geppetto
is not here! – cries Pinocchio.

– Da ist ein Loch in meiner Tasche! Das Geld, das ich Geppetto bringen will, ist nicht hier! – schreit Pinocchio.

Seite 23

But suddenly his nose begins to grow.
– Are you sure? Don't lie. Where is your money? – the Blue Fairy asks.

Doch plötzlich beginnt seine Nase zu wachsen.
– Bist du sicher? Lüg nicht. Wo ist dein Geld? – fragt die Blaue Fee.

Seite 24

– I don't know. It's not in my pocket anymore! – replies Pinocchio.
His nose goes on growing.

– Ich weiß nicht. Es ist nicht mehr in meiner Tasche! – antwortet Pinocchio. Seine Nase wächst weiter.

Seite 25

The Blue Fairy laughs: – When you tell a lie, your nose grows!
So Pinocchio promises not to tell any more lies.

Die Blaue Fee lacht: – Wenn du lügst, wächst deine Nase!
Da verspricht Pinocchio, nicht mehr zu lügen.

Seite 26

– Go home and be a good boy! – the Blue Fairy says.
Pinocchio thanks the Fairy and runs home.

– Geh nach Hause und sei ein guter Junge! – sagt die Blaue Fee.
Pinocchio dankt der Fee und läuft nach Hause.

Seite 27

But on the way he meets a boy. – Come to the Land of Toys with me! – he says. – Nobody goes to school there and you can play all day long!

Doch auf dem Weg trifft er einen Jungen. – Komm ins Spielzeugland mit mir! – sagt er. – Niemand geht dort zur Schule, und du kannst den ganzen Tag spielen!

Seite 28
– Don't listen to him – says Jiminy Cricket.

– Hör nicht auf ihn – sagt Jiminy Grille.

Seite 29
– We can take the carriage this evening – says the boy.

– Wir können heute Abend die Kutsche nehmen – sagt der Junge.

Seite 30
Pinocchio forgets all the promises to his father and to the Fairy.
They jump up in the carriage to the Land of Toys.

Pinocchio vergisst alle Versprechen, die er seinem Vater und der Fee gegeben hat.
Sie springen in die Kutsche zum Spielzeugland.

Seite 31
– Life is great here! No books, no lessons and we can play all the time! – cries Pinocchio.

– Das Leben ist herrlich hier! Keine Bücher, kein Unterricht, und wir können die ganze Zeit spielen! – schreit Pinocchio.

Seite 32
One day Pinocchio notices he has long, hairy ears …

Eines Tages merkt Pinocchio, dass er lange, haarige Ohren hat …

Seite 33
– You are turning into a donkey! – says Jiminy Cricket.
– I want to go home! – cries Pinocchio.

– Du verwandelst dich in einen Esel! – sagt Jiminy Grille.
– Ich will nach Hause! – schreit Pinocchio.

Seite 34
– Jump into the sea and escape from here! – says Jiminy Cricket.

– *Spring ins Meer und fliehe von hier! – sagt Jiminy Grille.*

Seite 35
So they jump into the dark sea and swim in the waves.

Da springen sie in das dunkle Meer und schwimmen in den Wellen.

Seite 36
Then they see a light in the dark.

Dann sehen sie ein Licht in der Dunkelheit.

Seite 37
They swim and swim right into the whale's mouth.
– We are inside a whale! – cries Jiminy Cricket.

Sie schwimmen und schwimmen, direkt ins Maul des Wals.
– Wir sind in einem Wal! – schreit Jiminy Grille.

Seite 38
– Pinocchio! – a voice calls. – What? But it's you, dad! –
cries Pinocchio so happy to see Geppetto.

– Pinocchio! – ruft eine Stimme. – Was? Aber das bist ja du, Papa! –
schreit Pinocchio, so glücklich, Geppetto zu sehen.

Seite 39
– We must get out of here and swim to land! – Pinocchio says.
When the whale opens its mouth, they get out.

– Wir müssen hier raus und an Land schwimmen! – sagt Pinocchio.
Als der Wal sein Maul öffnet, gelangen sie hinaus.

Seite 40

Pinocchio swims and pulls Geppetto.
When they reach dry land, they are very tired.

Pinocchio schwimmt und zieht Geppetto mit.
Als sie trockenes Land erreichen, sind sie sehr müde.

Seite 41

Finally they get home and immediately fall asleep.

Endlich kommen sie nach Hause und schlafen sofort ein.

Seite 42

The next day they wake up and the Blue Fairy is there.
– Look in the mirror! – she says to Pinocchio.

Am nächsten Tag wachen sie auf, und die Blaue Fee ist da.
– Schau in den Spiegel! – sagt sie zu Pinocchio.

Seite 43

Pinocchio is a real boy with blue eyes and brown hair.
– Oh, my son! – cries Geppetto with joy.

Pinocchio ist ein richtiger Junge mit blauen Augen und braunem Haar.
– Oh, mein Sohn! – ruft Geppetto voll Freude.

Seite 44

– You are a good boy: this is your reward! – says the Blue Fairy.

– Du bist ein guter Junge: Das ist deine Belohnung! – sagt die Blaue Fee.

Seite 45

Pinocchio and Geppetto are very happy and they jump and laugh together!

Pinocchio und Geppetto sind sehr glücklich, und sie hüpfen und
lachen zusammen!

 makes a  out of a piece of  . The puppet is alive and Geppetto gives him a spelling  to go to  .

 sells the spelling book to buy a  for a puppet show. Fire Eater gives Pinocchio some  to take to Geppetto. But Pinocchio tells a  and a  about his good fortune. They take

Pinocchio to a Magic and he buries the money. The next day the money is gone. The arrives and Pinocchio lies to her, so his begins to grow very long. On the way home he meets a and he follows him to the Land of Toys. Here Pinocchio starts growing long like a . He runs away and jumps into the . He swims inside a and meets Geppetto. They arrive home and the Blue Fairy turns Pinocchio into a real .

Find the differences

Look carefully at the two pictures and find the 5 differences.

Schau dir die zwei Bilder genau an und finde die 5 Unterschiede.

Find the words

Find the 4 words from the story!

Finde die 4 Wörter aus der Geschichte!

FOX

CAT

WHALE

PUPPET

A	P	I	L	V	P
Y	F	O	X	C	U
U	B	N	A	K	P
H	T	J	C	D	P
S	W	H	A	L	E
Z	G	W	T	E	T
R	Q	O	X	F	M

Join the numbers

Join the numbers from one to eighteen!

Verbinde die Zahlen von eins bis achtzehn!

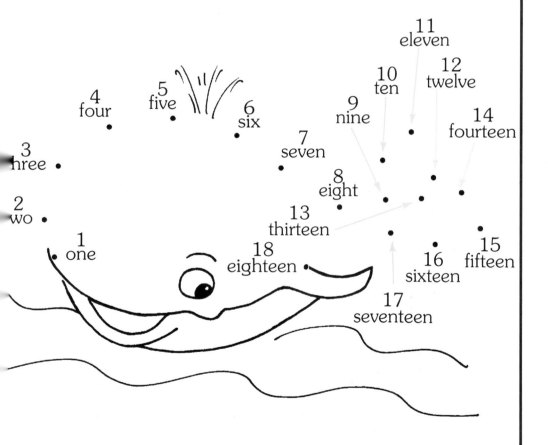

11 eleven
10 ten
12 twelve
4 four
5 five
6 six
9 nine
14 fourteen
3 hree
7 seven
8 eight
13 thirteen
2 wo
1 one
18 eighteen
16 sixteen
15 fifteen
17 seventeen

THIS IS A W _ _ _ _ _
IN THE SEA!

Match the words with the pictures

Ordne den Wörtern die Bilder zu!

BLUE FAIRY

PINOCCHIO

FIRE EATER

GEPPETTO

Crossword

Kreuzwort-
rätsel

Maze

Help Pinocchio to reach
the carriage to the Land of Toys!

*Labyrinth: Hilf Pinocchio, die Kutsche
zum Spielzeugland zu erreichen!*

A little dictionary

BOY: JUNGE   • • • **Nomen** • • •

CARPENTER: TISCHLER, SCHREINER

CARRIAGE: KARREN, KUTSCHE

CAT: KATZE, KATER

COAT: JACKE

CRICKET: GRILLE

DONKEY: ESEL

FAIRY: FEE

FIELD: FELD

FOX: FUCHS

LIE: LÜGE

MOUTH: MUND, MAUL

NOSE: NASE

POCKET: TASCHE

PUPPET: PUPPE

SCHOOL: SCHULE

SHOW: THEATER, VORSTELLUNG, SCHAUSPIEL

SON: SOHN

WHALE: WAL

WOOD: HOLZ

EMPTY: LEER   • • • **Adjektive** • • •

GOOD: GUT

HAPPY: GLÜCKLICH

POOR: ARM

TIRED: MÜDE

(TO) BURY: VERGRABEN • • • **Verben** • • •

(TO) BUY: KAUFEN

(TO) CRY: SCHREIEN, WEINEN

(TO) ESCAPE: FLIEHEN

(TO) FOLLOW: FOLGEN

(TO) GIVE: GEBEN

(TO) JUMP: HÜPFEN

(TO) GROW: WACHSEN

(TO) LIE: LÜGEN

(TO) MEET: TREFFEN, BEGEGNEN

(TO) PLAY: SPIELEN

(TO) SELL: VERKAUFEN

(TO) SWIM: SCHWIMMEN

Für die italienische Originalausgabe:
© 2007 Giunti Editore S.p.A., Firenze – Milano / Italia
Herausgegeben von Gabriella Ballarin

© 2010 Schwager & Stejnlein Verlag GmbH
Emil-Hoffmann-Straße 1, D-50996 Köln
Deutscher Text von Barbara Heller
Illustrationen von Giulio Peranzoni
Gesamtherstellung: Schwager & Steinlein Verlag GmbH
Alle Rechte vorbehalten

Art. Nr. 13863
ISBN 978-3-86775-863-5
www.schwager-steinlein-verlag.de